Planetarium

Julie Murray

Abdo Kids Junior
is an Imprint of Abdo Kids
abdobooks.com

Abdo
FIELD TRIPS
Kids

abdobooks.com

Published by Abdo Kids, a division of ABDO, P.O. Box 398166, Minneapolis, Minnesota 55439.
Copyright © 2020 by Abdo Consulting Group, Inc. International copyrights reserved in all countries.
No part of this book may be reproduced in any form without written permission from the publisher.
Abdo Kids Junior™ is a trademark and logo of Abdo Kids.

Printed in the United States of America, North Mankato, Minnesota.

102019

012020

THIS BOOK CONTAINS
RECYCLED MATERIALS

Photo Credits: Alamy, iStock, Media Bakery, Shutterstock

Production Contributors: Teddy Borth, Jennie Forsberg, Grace Hansen

Design Contributors: Christina Doffing, Candice Keimig, Dorothy Toth

Library of Congress Control Number: 2019941204
Publisher's Cataloging-in-Publication Data

Names: Murray, Julie, author.

Title: Planetarium / by Julie Murray

Description: Minneapolis, Minnesota : Abdo Kids, 2020 | Series: Field trips | Includes online
    resources and index.

Identifiers: ISBN 9781532188756 (lib. bdg.) | ISBN 9781532189241 (ebook) | ISBN 9781098200220
    (Read-to-Me ebook)

Subjects: LCSH: Planetarium--Juvenile literature. | Stargazing--Juvenile literature. | Telescopes--Juvenile
    literature. | School field trips--Juvenile literature.

Classification: DDC 371.384--dc23

Table of Contents

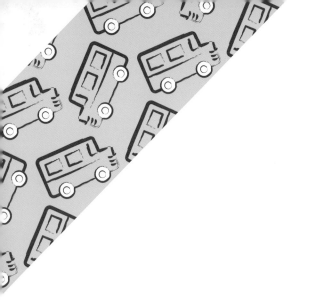

Planetarium

It's field trip day. The class is going to the planetarium.

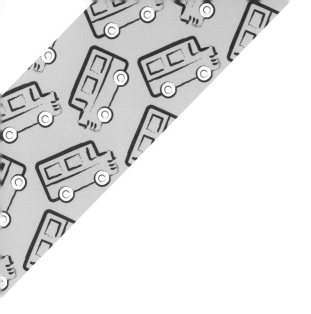

It is like a theater.

The ceiling is a dome.

The kids will learn about the night sky.

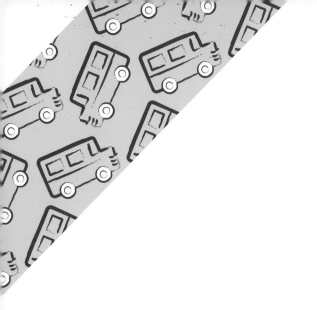

Sam finds his seat.

It gets dark.

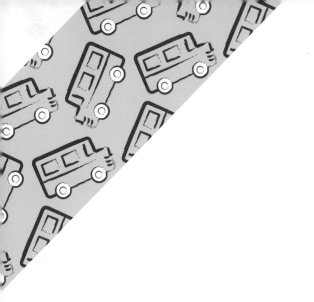

Sara looks up. She sees the sun. It is a big star!

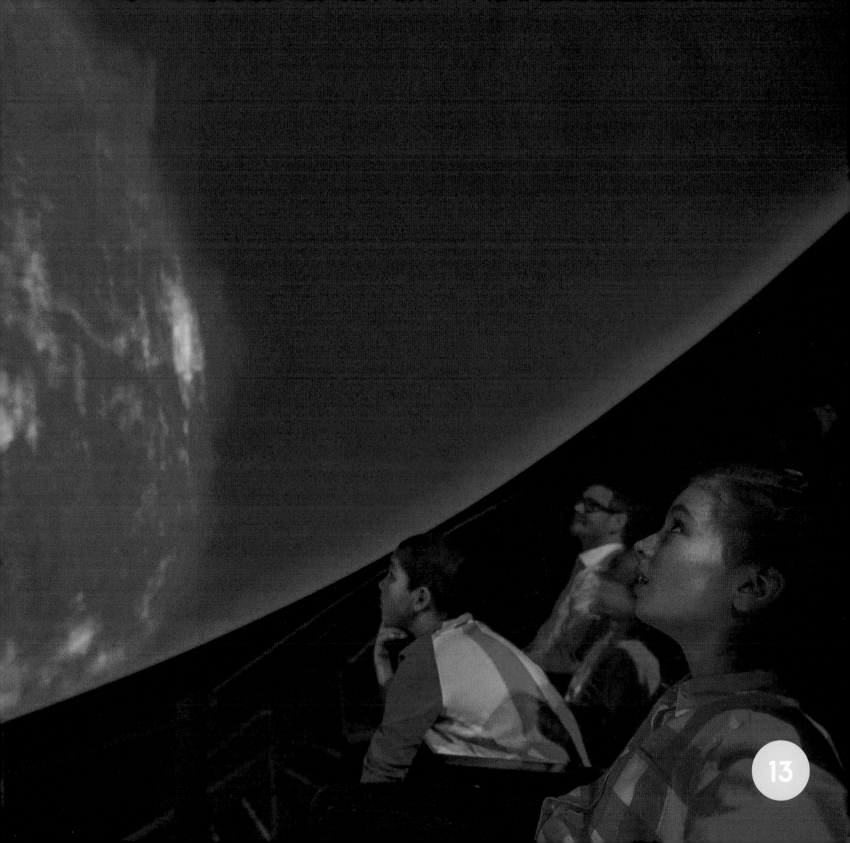

The class learns about the stars.

They learn about the planets.

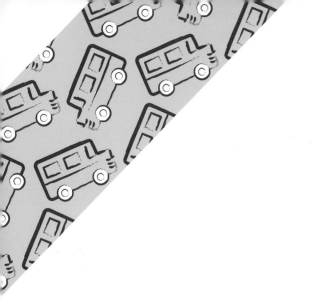

Evan sees the zodiac signs.

17

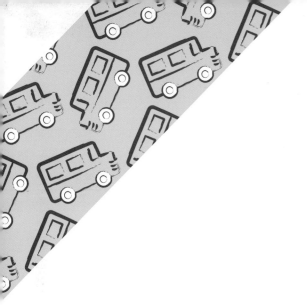

Ava finds Mars. It is big
and red.

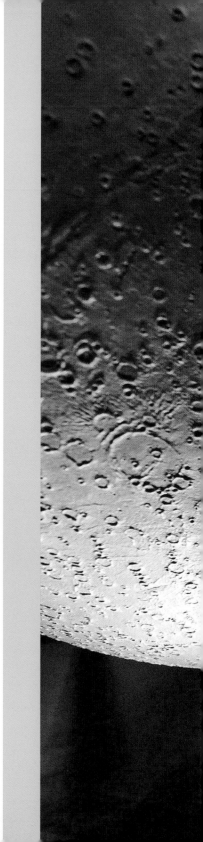

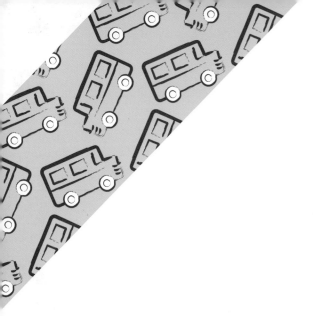

Have you been to

a planetarium?

Things You Can Learn About at the Planetarium

galaxies

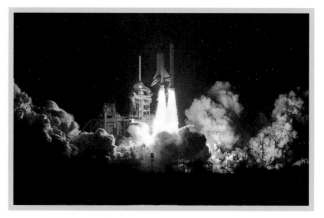

NASA missions

planets

stars

Glossary

dome
a rounded roof or ceiling on a room or building.

zodiac
an imaginary belt divided into 12 equal parts. Each part is named for a constellation that appears in the belt.

Index

Abdo Kids ONLINE

FREE! ONLINE MULTIMEDIA RESOURCES

Visit **abdokids.com** to access crafts, games, videos, and more!

Use Abdo Kids code

FPK8756

or scan this QR code!